The Gettysburg Address

DAVID & PATRICIA ARMENTROUT

Rourke
Publishing LLC
Vero Beach, Florida 32964

DOCUMENTS THAT SHAPED THE NATION

www.rourkepublishing.com

PHOTO CREDITS: Cover Scene and pg 33 © North Wind Picture Archives Pages 36 and 37 © James P. Rowan. Title Page © PhotoDisc, Inc. Page 15 Courtesy of the Department of the Interior. Page 19 Courtesy of the National Park Service. All other images from the Library of Congress

Title page: *Cannons at the Gettysburg National Military Park*

Editor: Frank Sloan

Cover and page design by Nicola Stratford

Library of Congress Cataloging-in-Publication Data

Armentrout, David, 1962-
  The Gettysburg address / David and Patricia Armentrout.
    p. cm. -- (Documents that shaped the nation)
  Includes text of: The Gettysburg address / Abraham Lincoln.
  Includes bibliographical references and index.
  ISBN 1-59515-232-6
 1. Lincoln, Abraham, 1809-1865. Gettysburg address--Juvenile literature.
2. United States--History--Civil War, 1861-1865--Juvenile literature. I.
Armentrout, Patricia, 1960- II. Lincoln, Abraham, 1809-1865. Gettysburg
address. III. Title.
IV. Series: Armentrout, David, 1962- Documents that shaped the nation.
  E475.55.A755 2004
  973.7'092--dc22

2004014417

Printed in the USA
CG

TABLE OF CONTENTS

THE GETTYSBURG ADDRESS

On November 19, 1863, President Lincoln sat on a red, white, and blue decorated platform, waiting for his turn to speak. He was with a crowd of thousands who had come to help dedicate a new national cemetery. The place was Gettysburg, Pennsylvania, where four months before a brutal battle had been fought.

President Lincoln had a lot on his mind. The nation was in the midst of a Civil War. The president made time, though, to leave his duties in Washington, D.C., and to write and rewrite a speech that would never be forgotten. Others spoke that day, some at great length, but the president's speech, known as the Gettysburg Address, was short and to the point.

An 1863 photograph of President Abraham Lincoln

BEFORE THE CIVIL WAR

How did the United States become divided and end up in a Civil War? The war erupted after years of Americans arguing over the rights of state and federal governments. Much of the arguing had to do with slavery in America.

From the time Jamestown Colony was settled in the 1600s, to the pre-Civil War period of the 1800s, the United States had experienced a period of great expansion. The size of the United States had doubled with the Louisiana

Purchase. The Erie Canal provided water transportation from New York City to the Great Lakes. Millions of Europeans were **emigrating** to America. Many of them settled in the North, where cities, factories, and other businesses sprang up alongside the expanding railroads. The country as a whole enjoyed a booming economy.

A ship full of people waiting to depart for America

A cotton plantation on the Mississippi River

In the South, the big business was **agriculture**. The livelihood of Southerners depended on the growth of their crops, which grew year round in the warm climate. **Plantation** owners had slaves who worked the land. They planted and harvested crops such as rice, sugar, tobacco, and cotton.

Early slaves in America were actually indentured servants: people who were under contract to work for a specific period of time, without pay, in exchange for a free passage to another country. Many were poor white Englishmen looking for a better life in America.

SLAVERY IN AMERICA

In 1619, a Dutch merchant ship loaded with Africans put in at Jamestown. There, the Africans were traded for food, and the slave trade began in America. Slavery resulted in increased crop production in the South and therefore an increase in exports.

Many slave laws were enacted in the 1600s. For example, in 1641, the Massachusetts Colony legalized slavery.

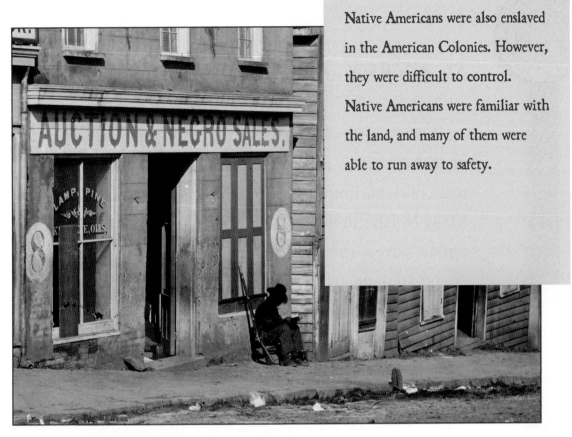

A slave auction house in Atlanta in 1864

This meant Africans were no longer indentured servants, they were **chattel** slaves—legal property of their owners. The following year the Virginia colony imposed fines on anyone who helped runaway slaves. By 1790, slavery was legal in every state. According to the first U.S. **Census**, there were 757,000 Blacks in the United States and only 9 percent were free. More than 50 percent of the slaves lived in Virginia and Maryland.

Slaves of rebel General Thomas Drayton at Hilton Head, South Carolina

SLAVERY AND POLITICS

By the 1850s, all states north of Maryland had **abolished** slavery and were considered free states. The issue of rights and slavery became a political nightmare. Many Northerners pressured the federal government to outlaw slavery throughout the Union. They said, "all men are created equal," just as it was written in the Declaration of Independence.

ESTATE SALE!

BY ORDER OF EXECUTOR.

By LOUIS D. DeSAUSSURE.

On Wednesday, 19th Inst.

AT 11 O'CLOCK, A. M. WILL BE SOLD IN

CHARLESTON, SO. CAROLINA,

AT

MESSRS. RYAN & SON'S MART,

IN CHALMERS STREET,

By order of the Executor of the late Mr. and Mrs. WM. BARNWELL,

A PRIME GANG OF

67 NEGROES,

Accustomed to the Culture of Sea Island Cotton and Provisions,

IN BEAUFORT DISTRICT. Amongst whom are several

HOUSE SERVANTS.

CONDITIONS.—One-third Cash; balance by Bond, bearing interest from day of sale, payable in two equal Annual Instalments, to be secured by a Mortgage of the Negroes, and approved Personal Security. Purchasers to pay for papers.

Slave cabins in Savannah, Georgia

Slavery helped make Southern plantation owners rich. Southerners argued that slaves were their property, and the Constitution protected a citizen's rights to own property. Their state representatives argued with the federal government saying that if the U.S. government passed laws to abolish slavery, their way of life would change forever.

An advertisement for a slave sale listing slaves' ages and abilities

SECESSION

The 1860 presidential election was all about slavery. Candidates were forced to take sides. Lincoln was the Republican Party's candidate. Republicans opposed slavery in all new territories. Still, Southerners feared their right to keep slaves would soon be taken away, so they threatened to **secede**.

A late 1850s portrait of Abraham Lincoln

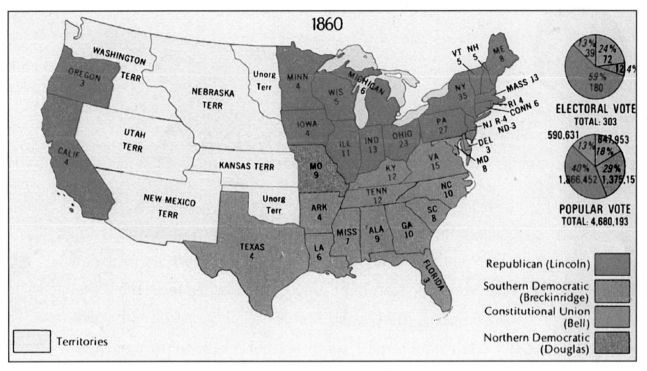

A political map of 1860 showing Abraham Lincoln winning the election

Lincoln, of course, won the election. He tried to convince the South that he would not abolish slavery, but Southerners felt they no longer had a strong voice in the government. On December 20, 1860, South Carolina seceded from the Union. Later Mississippi, Florida, Alabama, Georgia, Louisiana, and Texas followed.

Southerners who organized campaigns to secede from the Union were called Fire-eaters.

THE CIVIL WAR BEGINS

In February of 1861, the states that seceded formed a new nation called the Confederate States of America. They named Jefferson Davis as their temporary president. On March 4, Abraham Lincoln was sworn in as the 16th President of the United States.

Meanwhile, the Union thought it best to protect their property in the South. Major Robert Anderson brought about 90 troops to Fort Sumter, a small fortification on an island in Charleston Harbor. The South brought in forces as well, and under the command of General Pierre Gustave Toutant Beauregard, they encircled the fort with cannons.

Fort Sumter under Confederate cannonfire

On April 11, General Beauregard demanded Major Anderson's surrender, but Anderson refused. On April 12, at 4:30 A.M., troops led by General Beauregard opened fire on Fort Sumter, and the American Civil War began.

Major Anderson and his troops held Fort Sumter for months before surrendering to General Beauregard.

The bombardment of Confederate guns on Fort Sumter lasted for a day and a half. Remarkably, there were no deaths due to gunfire. However, during the formal surrender ceremony, a Union **artillerist** was killed when a cannon prematurely fired during a salute.

On April 14th, Major Anderson and his troops gave up the fort and were put on ships bound for New York.

Union troops defending Fort Sumter

Fort Sumter was dedicated as a National Monument in 1948. The five-sided fortification was built on a bed of rock, sand, and shells. The walls are about 5 feet (1.5 m) thick and still show the damage caused by Confederate cannon balls.

A TERRIBLE WAR

After the battle of Fort Sumter, the war between the North and South had officially begun. President Lincoln called for thousands of troops for his Union Army.

Major battles between Union and Confederate forces continued, but neither side seemed to be winning the war.

It was a terrible time. Soldiers suffered from lack of food and dehydration. Thousands of men died during the first two years, many from sickness or wounds that couldn't be attended to properly.

By this time there were 11 Confederate States and four border states. The border states—Missouri, Kentucky, Maryland, and Delaware—were slave states, but still loyal to the Union. One reason Lincoln did not free the slaves was because he feared the border states might secede. He needed troops and support from the border states for his Union army.

General Ulysses S. Grant leads a charge on rebel soldiers at the Battle of Pittsburgh, Tennessee.

BLACK SOLDIERS AND FREE SLAVES

Before the war, the United States Congress did not allow free Blacks or escaped slaves to join the Union Army.

What happened next would change the Union forever. President Lincoln decided it was in the Union's best interest to free the slaves in the South. It was his hope that after freeing the slaves, they would head north and join the Union forces. The president was right. He made a formal announcement on January 1, 1863 to free slaves in Confederate controlled states. This announcement was Lincoln's famous **Emancipation Proclamation**. After the formal emancipation of slaves, thousands of Blacks answered the call to arms.

When slaves learned of their freedom (owners did not tell them), they escaped to the North. Northerners were split on Lincoln's act of emancipation. Some welcomed the fact that their forces were increasing, while others hated the idea that they were fighting a war about slavery instead of a war to save the Union.

This photograph from the Civil War collection of the Library of Congress shows a military band from the 107th U.S. Colored Infantry at Fort Corcoran in Arlington, Virginia.

THE BATTLE OF GETTYSBURG

The summer of 1863 came, and forces on both sides were tired. Confederate General Robert E. Lee wanted desperately to win a battle on Northern soil.

Word spread that Lee was moving troops north. The Union took measures to protect the capital, but General Lee did not take his soldiers to Washington D.C. Instead,

The Battle of Gettysburg lasted three days. Union losses were estimated at 23,000 and Confederate losses were estimated at 28,000.

he split them up and moved them into
Pennsylvania. His plans were to take
Harrisburg, Pennsylvania's capital, and
then move on to Philadelphia
and Baltimore.

On June 30, Union General
George Meade, who had just been
appointed leader of the Union
forces the day before, sent a
small band of Union troops to
scout the area around Gettysburg.
Union troops entered Gettysburg
and learned General Lee also
had men in the area. General
Lee's cavalry spotted the Union
soldiers on a ridge outside of town.
The next morning, July 1,
Confederate forces attacked the
Union army, and the bloodiest
battle of the Civil War began.

Union General George G. Meade

General Meade brought more than 80,000 troops into Gettysburg that first night. General Lee had 75,000 troops. The next day they fought for prime positions around the town. Fighting occurred at areas that became known as Little Round Top, Peach Orchard, and Wheat Field. By nightfall on that second day Union troops were forced back to Cemetery Hill, but they managed to keep Confederate forces at bay.

On July 3, General Lee decided to make a direct attack on the Union line. Lee ordered Major General George Pickett to attack General Meade's battle line. Thousands of Confederate forces charged toward Union cannons. Union artillery blasted away as Confederate troops moved toward them. When the two armies finally met, the soldiers fought hand to hand. Known as Pickett's Charge, it was the last attempt by Confederate forces to win the battle. In the end, there were 51,000 dead soldiers, along with 5,000 dead horses and 569 tons of expended ammunition strewn across the battlefield. The Battle of Gettysburg was the largest and bloodiest battle ever fought on American soil.

Confederate General Robert E. Lee

DAVID WILLS

The aftermath of the Battle of Gettysburg was devastating. The landscape was dotted with shallow graves. David Wills, a citizen of Gettysburg, thought something special needed to be done. He wrote the governor of Pennsylvania asking for a cemetery for the soldiers. The governor raised money for the cemetery, and it was designed and built close to Cemetery Ridge, the town's small burial ground. When the work was complete, thousands of soldiers were brought there to be buried.

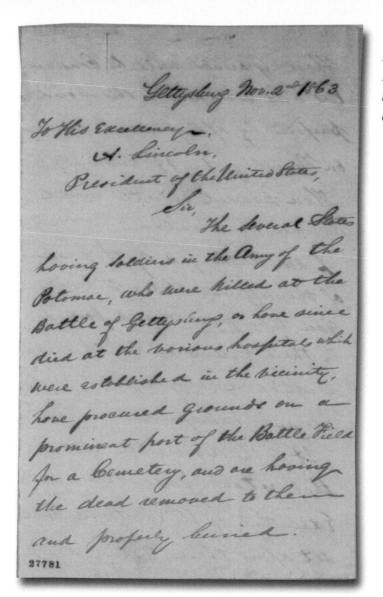

David Wills's letter to Lincoln asking the president to speak at the Gettysburg dedication ceremony

Mr. Wills also arranged a dedication ceremony for the cemetery. He asked many important people to speak at the dedication. He wrote President Lincoln asking him to come to Gettysburg.

After the war had ended, Confederate soldiers were moved to burial grounds in the South.

A Civil War Ambulance Corps removing wounded from the field

ARRIVING AT GETTYSBURG

The night before President Lincoln left for Gettysburg, he began working on his speech. He knew Edward Everett was planning to speak before him. Everett was a famous **orator** who often spoke at great length. The president decided to make his speech short.

Lincoln arrived by train the following day, and he was taken to Mr. Wills's home. There he met Mr. Everett. They had dinner together with other **dignitaries**. A parade to the cemetery began early the next day. The president rode on horseback and was joined by governors, congressmen, and generals.

The parade ended at the cemetery where the speakers all sat on a platform in the middle of what had once been a battlefield. A band played and a choir sang. Mr. Everett spoke for two hours, and then it was the president's turn.

Edward Everett spoke for two hours before Lincoln's speech at the Gettysburg Cemetery dedication.

LINCOLN'S ADDRESS AT GETTYSBURG

The president rose from his seat and addressed the thousands who stood before him.

Four score and seven years ago our fathers brought forth on this continent, a new nation, conceived in Liberty, and dedicated to the proposition that all men are created equal.

Now we are engaged in a great civil war, testing whether that nation, or any nation so conceived and so dedicated, can long endure. We are met on a great battle-field of that war. We have come to dedicate a portion of that field, as a final resting place for those who here gave their lives that that nation might live. It is altogether fitting and proper that we should do this.

But, in a larger sense, we can not dedicate -- we can not consecrate -- we can not hallow -- this ground. The brave men, living and dead, who struggled here, have consecrated it, far above our poor power to add or detract. The world will little note, nor long remember what we say here, but it can never forget what they did here. It is for us the living, rather, to be dedicated here to the unfinished work

President Lincoln giving his famous Gettysburg Address

which they who fought here have thus far so nobly advanced. It is rather for us to be here dedicated to the great task remaining before us -- that from these honored dead we take increased devotion to that cause for which they gave the last full measure of devotion -- that we here highly resolve that these dead shall not have died in vain -- that this nation, under God, shall have a new birth of freedom -- and that government of the people, by the people, for the people, shall not perish from the earth.

AFTER GETTYSBURG

Many people applauded Lincoln's speech at the dedication. Edward Everett later wrote to the president saying, "I should be glad, if I could flatter myself that I came as near to the central idea of the occasion, in two hours, as you did in two minutes."

General Lee surrenders to General Grant at the Appomattox Court House in Virginia on April 9, 1865.

However, some did not accept Lincoln's speech with as much praise. The criticism came mostly from Southern newspapers.

Lincoln returned to Washington, D.C., and to his duties of the ongoing war. Battles continued to rage until April 9, 1865. The war ended when General Lee surrendered to General Ulysses S. Grant at the Appomattox Court House in Virginia.

More than 620,000 Americans were killed in battle or died from illness in the Civil War.

An illustration published in 1865 of President Lincoln and Union Generals William Tecumseh Sherman, Philip Henry Sheridan, and Ulysses S. Grant

GETTYSBURG NATIONAL MILITARY PARK

The Gettysburg National Military Park was established February 11, 1895. Almost two million people visit the park each year. It has 1,400 monuments, markers, and memorials dedicated to the armies that fought at Gettysburg. The park also has a museum that displays Civil War relics.

A monument to General Meade at Gettysburg National Military Park

Park visitors experience what life was like for Civil War soldiers. Visitors tour the battlefield and stand in the spot where President Lincoln gave his Gettysburg Address.

The Soldiers' National Cemetery is part of the National Military Park. More than 7,000 soldiers are buried in the cemetery. More than 3,500 of those buried there died in the Civil War. Monuments and cannons throughout the cemetery remind visitors that the cemetery was once a battlefield.

The Lincoln Speech Memorial was erected on the site where President Lincoln made his Gettysburg Address.

THE DOCUMENTS

There are five known copies, or drafts, of the Gettysburg Address. Two drafts are kept at the Library of Congress in Washington, D.C. The first one is believed to be Lincoln's first draft and is often called the Nicolay copy. Lincoln gave this draft to his private secretary, John George Nicolay. It remained in Nicolay's possession until his death, and it was then transferred to John Hay.

The first page of the Nicolay copy was written in ink on Executive Mansion (White House) stationery. The second page was written in pencil on foolscap, a lined linen paper. Because of the different papers, it is likely the president wrote his speech while still in Washington and changed or finished it after arriving in Gettysburg.

Some scholars believe the Nicolay copy was the one the president read from at Gettysburg. However, some argue that the copy Lincoln read from was probably lost, because some words and phrases on the Nicolay draft did not match what was said that day.

A photograph of the first draft, or Nicolay copy, of the Gettysburg Address

John Hay, also a private secretary of Lincoln's, was given a second draft by the president. Lincoln most likely wrote that copy after returning to Washington. John Hay's family donated the Hay and Nicolay copies to the Library of Congress in 1916.

The president wrote the other three copies long after his speech on November 19. One copy is at the Illinois State Historical Library. It was written for Edward Everett, the orator who spoke for two hours prior to Lincoln's address. The Bancroft copy was requested by George Bancroft and is kept at Cornell University. The last copy was made for Colonel Alexander Bliss, Bancroft's stepson. It is in the Lincoln Room of the White House.

John Hay and John Nicolay wrote a biography of Abraham Lincoln. The first 10 volumes, titled "Abraham Lincoln: A History," were published in 1890.

John Hay, assistant secretary to President Lincoln

PRESERVING THE GETTYSBURG ADDRESS

The Library of Congress had two state-of-the-art cases made to house their copies of the Gettysburg Address. A special vault was also built to store the cases.

42

The cases have stainless steel frames that are filled with low-moisture argon gas. The gas gets rid of oxygen inside the case, which can cause deterioration of the documents. The documents are suspended, without adhesive, between plexiglass, which filters out ultraviolet rays.

The Library of Congress took measures to preserve the

original drafts of the Gettysburg Address so they can be viewed and enjoyed for generations. The Nicolay draft is the one on exhibit at the Library of Congress Jefferson Building in Washington, D.C.

The Library of Congress in Washington, D.C.

TIME LINE

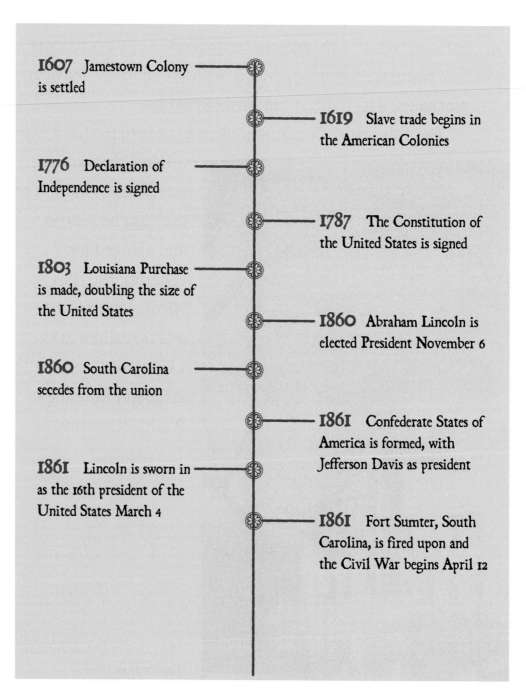

1607 Jamestown Colony is settled

1619 Slave trade begins in the American Colonies

1776 Declaration of Independence is signed

1787 The Constitution of the United States is signed

1803 Louisiana Purchase is made, doubling the size of the United States

1860 Abraham Lincoln is elected President November 6

1860 South Carolina secedes from the union

1861 Confederate States of America is formed, with Jefferson Davis as president

1861 Lincoln is sworn in as the 16th president of the United States March 4

1861 Fort Sumter, South Carolina, is fired upon and the Civil War begins April 12

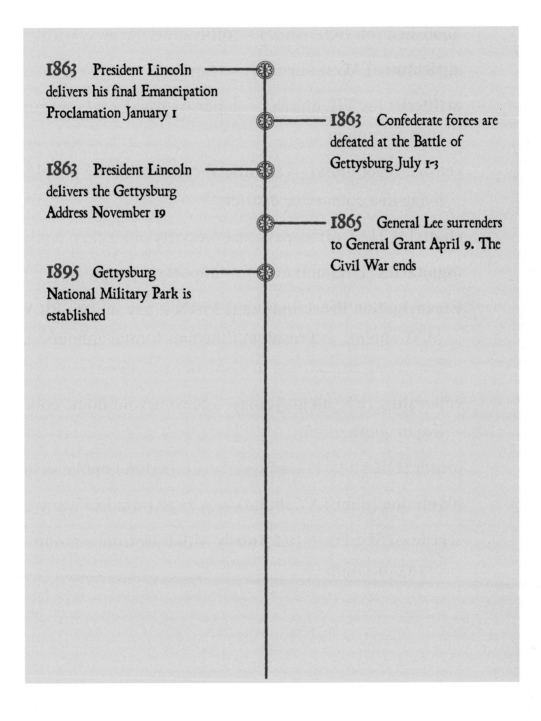

1863 President Lincoln delivers his final Emancipation Proclamation January 1

1863 Confederate forces are defeated at the Battle of Gettysburg July 1-3

1863 President Lincoln delivers the Gettysburg Address November 19

1865 General Lee surrenders to General Grant April 9. The Civil War ends

1895 Gettysburg National Military Park is established

GLOSSARY

abolished (uh BOL ished) — officially done away with

agriculture (AG ri kul chur) — farming

artillerist (ar TIL uh rist) — a person who fires large guns such as cannon

census (SEN suhss) — an official count of all the people living in a country or district

chattel (CHAT ul) — personal property other than land; slave

dignitaries (DIG ni tar eez) — important people

Emancipation Proclamation (i MAN si pay shuhn   PRAK leh MAY shuhn) — President Lincoln's formal announcement that freed slaves living in Confederate States

emigrating (EM uh grayt ing) — leaving your home country to live in another one

orator (OR uh tor) — a powerful and skillful public speaker

plantation (plan TAY shuhn) — a large farm in a warm climate

secede (si SEED) — to formally withdraw from a group or organization

FURTHER READING

King, David C. *The Battle of Gettysburg.*
    Blackbirch Marketing, 2001.

Murray, Aaron R. *Civil War Battles and Leaders.*
    Dorling Kindersley Publishing, 2004.

Stanchak, John. *Civil War.*
    Dorling Kindersley Publishing, 2000.

Tanaka, Shelley. *A Day That Changed America: Gettysburg.*
    Hyperion Press, 2003.

WEBSITES TO VISIT

www.loc.gov/exhibits/gadd/

www.historyplace.com/civilwar/

www.americancivilwar.info/

ABOUT THE AUTHORS

David and Patricia Armentrout have written many nonfiction books for young readers. They have had several books published for primary school reading. The Armentrouts live in Cincinnati, Ohio, with their two children.

INDEX